The Joy of Two Pianos

Favorite themes and pieces arranged for two pianos, four hands.
Edited by Denes Agay

Cover illustration by Janice Fried

Order Number: YK 21459
US International Standard Book Number: 0.8256.8076.X
UK International Standard Book Number: 0.7119.1657.8

Exclusive Distributors:
Music Sales Corporation
257 Park Avenue South, New York, New York 10010 USA
Music Sales Limited
8/9 Frith Street, London W1V 5TZ England
Music Sales Pty. Limited
120 Rothschild Street, Rosebery, Sydney, NSW 2018, Australia

Printed in the United States of America by
Vicks Lithograph and Printing Corporation

Yorktown Music Press, Inc.
New York/London/Sydney

2

Menuet

from the Little Notebook for Anna Magdalena Bach

Second piano part
by John Diercks

Johann Sebastian Bach
(1685–1750)

2nd time :

Two Ländler

1.

Arranged by Denes Agay

Wolfgang Amadeus Mozart
(1756–1791)

2.

No. 1 may be repeated

Sonatina

first movement

Second piano part by
Henry C. Timm

Muzio Clementi, Op. 36, No. 1
(1752–1832)

Two Stephen Foster Songs

Arranged by John Diercks

Stephen Foster
(1826–1864)

1.
Jeannie with the Light Brown Hair

12

2.
Oh! Susanna

Rondo all'Ungharese

from Piano Concerto in D Major

Arranged by Denes Agay

Franz Joseph Haydn
(1732–1809)

Russian Sailors' Dance

from the ballet "The Red Poppy"

Arranged by Denes Agay

Rheinhold Glière
(1875–1956)

37 Allegro

Meet Frankie and Johnny

Denes Agay

Liebesfreud

Love's Joy

Arranged by Denes Agay

Fritz Kreisler
(1875–1962)

Music Box Rag

Denes Agay

38

Chassidic Round Dance

from Mosaics: Six Piano Pieces on Jewish Themes

Denes Agay

Chit-Chat Polka

Arranged by Jean Reynolds Davis

Johann Strauss

48

The Joy of Two Pianos

Favorite themes and pieces arranged for two pianos, four hands.
Edited by Denes Agay

Cover illustration by Janice Fried

Order Number: YK 21459
US International Standard Book Number: 0.8256.8076.X
UK International Standard Book Number: 0.7119.1657.8

Exclusive Distributors:
Music Sales Corporation
257 Park Avenue South, New York, New York 10010 USA
Music Sales Limited
8/9 Frith Street, London W1V 5TZ England
Music Sales Pty. Limited
120 Rothschild Street, Rosebery, Sydney, NSW 2018, Australia

Printed in the United States of America by
Vicks Lithograph and Printing Corporation

Yorktown Music Press, Inc.
New York/London/Sydney

Menuet

from the Little Notebook for Anna Magdalena Bach

Second piano part
by John Diercks

Johann Sebastian Bach
(1685–1750)

* 2nd time :

4

Two Ländler

1.

Arranged by Denes Agay

Wolfgang Amadeus Mozart
(1756–1791)

2.

6

No. 1 may be repeated

Sonatina

first movement

Second piano part by
Henry C. Timm

Muzio Clementi, Op. 36, No. 1
(1752–1832)

Two Stephen Foster Songs

Arranged by John Diercks

Stephen Foster
(1826–1864)

1.

Jeannie with the Light Brown Hair

2.
Oh! Susanna

Rondo all'Ungharese

from Piano Concerto in D Major

Arranged by Denes Agay

Franz Joseph Haydn
(1732–1809)

Russian Sailors' Dance

from the ballet "The Red Poppy"

Arranged by Denes Agay

Rheinhold Glière
(1875–1956)

Meet Frankie and Johnny

Denes Agay

Liebesfreud

Love's Joy

Arranged by Denes Agay

Fritz Kreisler
(1875–1962)

Music Box Rag

Denes Agay

Chassidic Round Dance

from Mosaics: Six Piano Pieces on Jewish Themes

Denes Agay

Chit-Chat Polka

Arranged by Jean Reynolds Davis

Johann Strauss